BIGGER GOSPEL

CAESAR KALINOWSKI

BIGGER

LEARNING TO SPEAK, LIVE, AND ENJOY
THE GOOD NEWS IN EVERY AREA OF LIFE

GOSPEL

A PRACTICAL GUIDE FOR GROWING
IN GOSPEL FLUENCY

For more info or to find out about bulk discounts:
www.missiopublishing.com
©2017 Missio Publishing
published by Missio Publishing
ISBN 978-1-63587-392-4

Designer
Blake Berg

Missio
publishing

missiopublishing.com
caesarkalinowski.com

CONTENTS

ACKNOWLEDGEMENTS

Like is often the case in my life, God speaks to me through many people in many ways. If you are one of those people and you read something in this book that you taught me, I am grateful. I have tried to acknowledge you along the way as memory serves.

To my family, friends and all of the leaders around the world that I have hashed out these teachings with, for you, I am also very thankful.

The Gospel is so much bigger than I ever imagined!

INTRODUCTION

Have you wished you could share your Christian faith with others in a natural way without feeling awkward or preachy?

Have you ever longed for a faith that touched down more than just Sunday to Sunday leading up to one long afterlife?

I can relate.

When I first "got saved" my understanding of the gospel pretty much focused on getting out of hell and where I would spend my afterlife. It's true that when I put my faith in Jesus as my Lord and Savior I inherited eternal life with God. But I thought (and was taught) little about how this good news might actually affect *this* life. Here and now.

BIGGER GOSPEL

How does the gospel speak into my marriage and parenting, finances and identity? Is there "good news" about my job and time management too?

Well, there is. We can grow in our ability to naturally and confidently speak, live and enjoy the Gospel in every area of life. I call this *Gospel Fluency*[1].

WHAT IS GOSPEL FLUENCY?

While visiting the Czech Republic many times over the past ten years or so, I have learned little bits of their language slowly over time. When I try to speak, however, I ended up sounding more like a caveman uttering mispronounced words, ideas and comments in short, stunted bursts of uncertainty. The looks on their kind Czech faces confirmed my fears: they had very little idea what I was talking about! Not good.

I wonder if that is how we often sound to each other, and those who are not-yet believers, when we speak about Jesus and his Kingdom?

How "fluent" in the gospel are you?

BECOMING GOSPEL FLUENT

In order to be effectively equipped or teach others to be fluent in the gospel, we need to create a culture where it is normal to speak the gospel to each other regularly and naturally.

Every sin and issue that stands in the way of our faithfulness to God's design and Jesus' commands is ultimately a gospel

INTRODUCTION

issue. Since all sin is the outcome of unbelief in some aspect of what is true of God, we can learn to apply the truth about him and the Good News to the unbelief in every area of our lives. To do this, we must learn to trust God and others with our sin and the messiness of our lives. The foundation of a gospel-centered, missional life is the decision to offer God our plans in exchange for his plans. We must allow the truth about who God is, what he has done, and our new identity in Christ to inform all of life.

> See to it, brothers and sisters, that none of you has a sinful, unbelieving heart that turns away from the living God.
> *Hebrews 3:12*

Jesus' life and teaching always attracted a crowd; he was loved by the irreligious and outcast and hated by the moralistic, legalistic religious types. If our lives and proclamation of the gospel are not having a similar effect in our culture, then it is probably a different message we proclaim[2].

Problems with evangelism and discipleship (and life in community, for that matter) all stem from having a gospel that is too small. Either that, or we do not know how to communicate it in real-time in a way that is truly good news.

Let's get to work changing that.

There are several critical things we've learned, and steps we've taken, to grow in our gospel fluency. I want to share them with you now.

BIGGER GOSPEL

The first few chapters help set the stage (and till the ground of our hearts) for what will be a step-by-step process for growing in your gospel fluency.

We'll get started by asking three important and clarifying questions, starting with the first: *Discipleship or Evangelism?*

A FEW CLARIFYING QUESTIONS

CHAPTER 1

Discipleship or Evangelism?

The thought of going out and evangelizing people can seem scary and uncomfortable. Most folks I know would prefer to avoid it altogether and none of us love the "bullhorn" guy who stands on the street and hollars at people to repent.

Truthfully, I think many (probably most) Christians don't share their faith with any regularity because they somehow know that they are not all that fluent in the gospel. What they have to say does not sound like very good news. Almost no one I know sets out to look and sound stupid or be rejected. Not so much.

But how will anyone come to trust and love Jesus if they don't know him or have not heard and experienced the truth about him? (Romans 10:14)

Yet interestingly, Jesus' command in Matthew 28 was actually to go and *make disciples* who make disciples. Nothing mentioned here about evangelism.

So which is it? Which is more important, discipleship or evangelism?

Let's take a look.

WHICH CAME FIRST?

For many of us, we see evangelism as what happens–the words, events, activities etc.–that bring us (or others) to the point of belief or 'faith'. In contrast, we usually understand discipleship to be the process for growth in our Christian life after we've come to faith. Evangelism gets us in the door and then the work of discipleship begins.

Traditionally, it looks something like this:

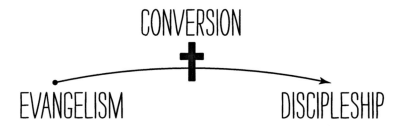

But let's look a little closer.

DISCIPLESHIP OR EVANGELISM?

ARE WE DOING THIS WHOLE THING OUT OF ORDER?

Another word for faith is "belief," and the Bible clearly teaches us that all sin comes from not believing what is true about God. (Romans 14:23)

Discipleship (or what is sometimes called sanctification) is the process of moving from unbelief to belief about what is true of God and the gospel, in absolutely *every area of life*. Jesus described it this way, "If you hold to my teaching, you are really my disciples."

Okay, pretty clear and simple.

But then he went on to say something really interesting: *"Then you will know the truth, and the truth will set you free"* (John 8:31-32). In Jesus' view, the whole thing *starts* with learning to follow him–becoming his disciple. Living in his ways.

As we enter that process, and as a result of it, our lives are transformed and we are set free from guilt, shame and the weight of sin. This is what discipleship is all about! According to Jesus, we are discipled to the truth that sets us free.

In my experience we have often done this whole process backwards. We expect people to first believe what we tell them is "the truth", and next say a "Jesus in their heart" prayer to be saved... and THEN we start to disciple them. But that is not what Jesus says here, nor is it what he modeled in his own life.

Did Jesus call his disciples to follow him and "do life" with him *after* they got saved?

Nope.

He called them to walk in his ways for three years as they came to know the truth and experience the Kingdom. This is what led to their transformation, their freedom.

So then, does what Jesus said and modeled look like this?

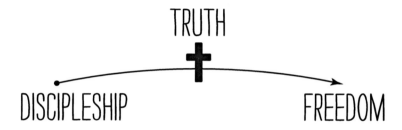

THIS IS IMPORTANT

Don't assume that the first move from unbelief to belief that happens in a person's life is always around the issue of their ultimate and utter sinfulness and need for a savior. As we engage people and treat them like family, their first shifts in belief may be in the areas of trust and grace and God's abundant generosity as experienced through us and in community.

I'll bet if we are honest with ourselves, our own faith journey had many shifts in belief about who God is and what he has done in and through his Son, before we came to believe we needed saving from our own sinful, rebellious choices.

We see that whether we are talking about our own hearts or the hearts and lives of our friends and neighbors, the process of discipleship (evangelism in its truest sense) can begin long before a confession of faith and continues throughout our entire lives. This is what it means to say that the gospel saves and sanctifies us.

AND ON IT GOES FROM THERE...

So then, just as you received Christ Jesus as Lord, continue to live your lives in him, rooted and built up in him, strengthened in the faith as you were taught...

Colossians 2:6,7

In the same way that we come to put our faith in Jesus by hearing and experiencing the gospel in community, we also continue to grow and mature by the light of that same gospel. This is a lifelong process. We are *always* in need of evangelism. In fact, discipleship can be simply understood as the ongoing evangelizing or "gospeling" of our hearts.

So maybe in fact it, what scripture teaches, most fully, looks more like this:

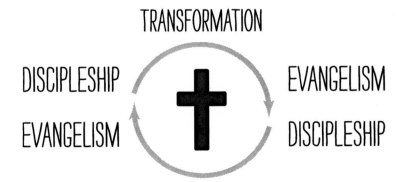

It is my strong opinion and experience that evangelism and discipleship were never meant to be two separate activities or practices.

Discipleship, again, is the process of moving from unbelief to belief, in the gospel, in every area of life. There is no true discipleship without the gospel in the center of it all. If evangelism is the applying of the gospel (good news) to every area of life, then discipleship is happening. One is not accomplished, nor does it exist, apart from the other.

So again, which is more important...discipleship or evangelism?

Yes.

SET FREE TO BE

When we begin to give ourselves permission to believe what Jesus said and modeled in this area we are set free. Evangelism is no longer an icky, weird and fearful "task" to be engaged in. Discipleship is moved out of the classroom and incorporates all of life. Inviting people to walk in the ways of Jesus with you, your family and community while the gospel is proclaimed and lived out accomplishes Jesus' full command.

The pressure is off my friend.

●◆●◆◆◆◆◆◆◆●

Now let's move to another important question as we prepare our hearts and lives to have greater gospel fluency and effectiveness: "Is Apologetics a Dirty Word?"

CHAPTER 2

Is Apologetics A Dirty Word?

I am not going to attempt to make a case for, or against, apologetics. It exists. It's a real thing. When used in the correct context with the right motives, it is a very important and necessary tool.

What I offer here is more of an observation and a gentle warning.

TWO CONVERSATIONS

Aaron: (not a Christian, but a gentle guy): *"I am so frustrated with politics and our government right now! I wish there was a better way."*

STEP 1 | A FEW CLARIFYING QUESTIONS

Mike: (a Christian who thinks this is a perfect opening to "witness" to his pal): *Well I'm sure glad that God is in control and powerful over everything, including our government.*

Aaron: *Well I don't know if that's true...look at the world and our country right now.*

Mike: *Come on Aaron, the Bible teaches that...XYZ... and if you look at the history of Israel and their leaders throughout history...XYZ and here's some facts about the numbers 7, 12 and 40...*

Aaron: *I'm not quite sure that makes a ton of sense to my sister trying to get healthcare right now.*

Mike: *Come on Aaron, the reason that so many people are hurting is that they reject the plain truth laid out in the Holy Scriptures. I just showed you proof.*

Aaron: *I guess we may not see things quite the same on this.*

Mike: *Why don't we get together so I can show you a chart I have that proves that governments throughout history...*

Aaron: *That's alright Mike, I think I'll pass.*

IS APOLOGETICS A DIRTY WORD?

A BETTER WAY

Right here you'd love it if I gave you the more loving and gospel-fluent version of how this conversation could have gone. Wouldn't you?

Keep reading. I'll get to it. First let's dive into what apologetics actually is and how it was used in the Bible.

I've noticed that one of the things that often put people off of talking about Christianity or the gospel to their friends is the fear of sounding like Mike, or being asked hard questions. People dread not being able to give adequate answers to these questions in a way that will sound like good news.

Doesn't the Bible contradict itself?

Is the Bible meant to be read literally?

What about other religions? Everyone else can't be totally wrong!

Isn't Christianity racist, sexist or homophobic?

Hasn't science disproved most of the Bible and Christianity?

If God is so good and powerful, then why do so many bad things happen?

I am sure you have a list of your own.

Responding to questions like these is commonly called *apologetics*. Apologetics comes from the Greek word apologia, which means "defense" or "answer". It is the word used in

1Peter 3:15 where we find the most commonly used case made for Christians to engage in apologetics:

> *In your hearts revere (set apart, sanctify) Christ as Lord.*
> *Always be prepared to give an answer [apologia] to*
> *everyone who asks you to give the reason for the hope*
> *that you have. But do this with gentleness and respect.*
>
> *1Peter 3:15*

The word apologia, while not meaning "apologetics" in the modern technical sense, does indicate that Christians are to be prepared to explain their confession of Jesus Christ as Lord[3].

That last part of that verse, though, is key: *with gentleness and respect*. Let's be sure to get our hearts in that position before we jump in.

Eugene Peterson's translation of this verse in *The Message* helps find the tone and posture we're looking for:

> *Through thick and thin, keep your hearts at attention, in*
> *adoration before Christ, your Master. Be ready to speak*
> *up and tell anyone who asks why you're living the way*
> *you are, and always with the utmost courtesy.*
>
> *1Peter 3:15 (MSG)*

This doesn't sound like a command to get into arguments to me.

IS APOLOGETICS A DIRTY WORD?

WAS APOLOGETICS IN THE NEW TESTAMENT?

Although perhaps none of the New Testament writings would fairly be classified as a formal apologetic exposition, some of them exhibit what we'll call "apologetic concerns".

The New Testament writers anticipate and answer objections, and look to demonstrate the credibility of the claims, testimony and credentials of Jesus. They especially focus on his resurrection as the historical foundation upon which Christianity (what it has come to be called) is built. And many of the New Testament writings are occupied with polemics against false teachings, in which the "apologetic concern" is to defend the gospel against distortion *from within the church.*

I think this is important for us to note: most of what we see is a defense of the gospel against perversion from *within* the existing faith community (Jewish or other) and the newly forming Church.

Remember, not much was written down and distributed yet.

There is one example that seems to differ, and yet should not be considered the "model du jour" for us now. Paul's address to the Athenians in Acts 17 is the only substantial example of an apology, or defense, directed to a non-Jewish audience in the New Testament (some also point to Acts 14:15-17). This one speech has traditionally been regarded as a paradigm or model of much of what we have come to call apologetics.

According to Luke (Acts 17:18), Paul's message of Jesus and the Resurrection was misunderstood as teaching new deities. Luke reports this accusation in terms nearly identical to those describing the Athenians' argument against Socrates in Plato's Apology (look it up), which strongly suggests that Luke sees Paul's speech here as a Christian counterpart to that Socratic discourse.

Heady stuff!

Challenged to explain his position by Stoic and Epicurean philosophers, Paul set his message in a rational context in which it would make sense to his philosophically minded audience. The speech was quite unlike those Paul delivered to Jewish audiences, which emphasized Jesus as the fulfillment of Old Testament messianic promises and quoted Old Testament proof texts liberally[4]. Paul is very aware of his audience and not merely quoting facts or trying to win an argument.

KNOW YOUR AUDIENCE

The hearer often dictates how our message of the good news is received, and therefore how it may need to be delivered. If you were to say to a three-year-old boy who's out helping his mother in the yard, *"Look at you, you're so big!"* he would probably be proud and receive your words as a compliment. But if you went up to the boy's mother at the exact same time and said to her, *"You're so big!"* she might punch you in the face.

Your audience matters.

Ask yourself:

- Do I know enough about this person and their story to give a loving response?

IS APOLOGETICS A DIRTY WORD?

- Do I have the necessary relationship and trust needed to get into this discussion?

- How will they "hear" what I am trying to communicate?

- Is this environment conducive for the conversation?

- Is this the right time to go there with him or her?

Apologetics is not a dirty word; it just depends on how you use it, to whom you're talking, and where and when.

THE BETTER CONVERSATION

Okay, so here's how a conversation between Christian Mike and his friend Aaron may have started:

Aaron: *I am so frustrated with politics and our government right now! I wish there was a better way.*

Mike: *I hear ya, Aaron, there is a lot of pain and division out there right now. I feel it inside of me too.*

Aaron: *I know you're a Christian, and we may have different views on this, but what's your thoughts on what we're experiencing right now?*

Mike: *I look in the mirror and want to see this perfect, always-loving guy looking back at me each day. But that's not always the case. I wonder if any real solutions to the fighting and division in our country need to start there. Inside of me...and you...first?*

STEP 1 | A FEW CLARIFYING QUESTIONS

Aaron: *I guess it makes sense that cities or countries and nations can't change if the people in them don't first begin to change.*

Mike: *I really do believe, Aaron, in a God who is love and calls us to love others in the way we love ourselves.*

Aaron: *Well that sounds good, but how the h*$* do we start doing that?!"*

Mike: *Why don't we get together for coffee or maybe a beer later this week and see if we can begin to find some good starting points. I'd really like to here more of your story too.*

Aaron: *Sounds cool. I also want to pick your brain a little about your fantasy league choices this season.*

Can you feel the difference? It's not weird; it's not an argument. A much better beginning to move toward deeper spiritual discussion with someone.

I'll bet you now want to hear the next conversation that Mike and Aaron have. Am I right? In Chapter 7 and 8 I will give you a tool and process to begin to ask the right questions in a situation like this in order to actually formulate a conversation that is gospel-centered and good news to the hearer.

IS APOLOGETICS A DIRTY WORD?

A MOTIVE CHECK

I'll close this chapter by coming back to 1 Peter 3:15:

In your hearts revere (set apart, sanctify) Christ as Lord. Always be prepared to give an answer (apologia) to everyone who asks you to give the reason for the hope that you have. But do this with gentleness and respect.

1 Peter 3:15

Notice that revering and sanctifying God is our first priority; offering a defense of our hope and faith is secondary and subsequent. This makes sense because our greatest love and affection is supposed to be directed toward God. Our obligation to serve others in love comes next (Matthew 22:37-39).

Biblical apologetics must proceed from our love for God and a desire to prioritize and glorify him as first priority in our lives. To "glorify" God is to show his true heart and what he is really like. Our motivation to love others, by sharing hope and the good news of the gospel, flows from that correct heart motivation.

So let's stop trying to argue people into the Kingdom.

The Aarons in your life will thank you for it.

⸻◆◆◆◆◆◆◆◆◆⸻

There's one more question we need to ask ourselves before moving on, and it is a big one: "What is the Gospel?"

CHAPTER **3**

What is the Gospel?

A few years ago I was with a group of Christians, many of them pastors and leaders, and I asked them the question, *"What is the Gospel?"* I waited for their response. I assumed that such a simple and obviously important question would net immediate and similar answers from everyone. Boy was I wrong!

I heard a dozen completely different answers and not one of them mentioned Jesus or sin or a cross. How could this be? And if a bunch of pastors could not give a good answer to this question, it made me wonder what kind of gospel message would be coming from the lips of the people they lead and serve?

WHAT IS THE GOSPEL?

The gospel is called the "good news" and it is particularly good news about our relationship with God. In a nutshell, we can sum it up this way:

The gospel is that God himself has come to rescue and renew creation in and through the work of Jesus Christ on our behalf[5].

Why does creation (which includes you and me) need rescuing?

Because of sin.

This may sound pretty heavy at first, but it's the truth. In order to understand the good news, we really do need to have a right understanding of sin.

Sin is making everything about ME. Sin is living life my way, for my fame and glory, instead of living God's way for God. We have all sinned and really need the gospel—we desperately need Jesus to rescue us from the penalty and effects of sin. (By the way... all sin comes from unbelief. We'll look deeply at this in Part 3.)

When we repent–change our mind and believe the truth about who God is, what he's accomplished and what is now true of us–then by faith, we believe that Jesus' life, death and resurrection has secured our rescue and restored us to a right relationship with God the Father. This good news is true now for us. Every area of life can begin to be restored back to the way God designed it to be.

> *It will make a weak man mighty. It will make a mighty man fall. It will fill your heart and hands or leave you with nothing at all. It's the eyes for the blind and legs for the lame. It is the love for hate and pride for shame. That's the power of the gospel.*
> *~Ben Harper*

Think about all the many things that were accomplished (restored) on your behalf by Jesus' perfect life, his death and resurrection...this is all VERY good news!

Reference	What is now true because of Jesus
John 5:24	death to life, no judgment, eternal life
2 Corinthians 5:17	new creation/identity, old has gone
Romans 5:1	peace with God
Romans 8:1	no condemnation
Romans 8:2	set free from law of sin and death
Ephesians 1:5	adopted as sons and daughters
Ephesians 3:16-18	indwelled Spirit, power, love of Christ
Colossians 3:1-4	died in Christ, raised in Christ, hidden in
1 John 4:7-12	we are loved
Revelation 12:10,11	accuser–Satan destroyed

IT GET'S EVEN BETTER!

The gospel is not just an ancient story about God's son dying on a cross two thousand years ago. The good news is much better than that!

The gospel *HAS* saved us from the penalty of sin.
The gospel *IS* saving us from the power of sin.
The gospel *WILL* save us from the presence of sin.

THE GOSPEL DID NOT *HAPPEN...*IT IS *HAPPENING!*

Like I said earlier, when I first "got saved" my understanding of the gospel was pretty much focused on my afterlife. And it is true, when I accepted Jesus' death in place of my own, my sins were forgiven and I inherited eternal life with God. But I thought little about the reality that because of his death and resurrection, Jesus enables me to say "no" to the power and pull of sin in my life NOW.

Sin has been put to death and through the power of Christ's indwelt Spirit. I can today, increasingly, live the life I was created to live. And there is a day that is coming when Jesus returns to put away all sin and sickness and destruction. Everything will be restored to the way God originally created it. The gospel is a past, present and future reality[6].

Entering into this fullness is not something you figure out or achieve. It's not a matter of being circumcised or keeping a long list of laws. No, you're already in — insiders — not through some secretive initiation rite but rather through what Christ has already gone through for you, destroying the power of sin. If it's an initiation ritual you're after, you've already been through it by submitting to baptism. Going under the water was a burial of your old life; coming up out of it was a resurrection, God raising you from the dead as he did Christ. When you were stuck in your old sin-dead life, you were incapable of responding to God. God brought you alive—right along with Christ! Think of it! All sins forgiven, the slate wiped clean, that old arrest warrant canceled and nailed to Christ's cross. He stripped all the spiritual tyrants in the universe of their sham authority at the Cross and marched them naked through the streets.

Colossians 2:11-15 (MSG)

In the next chapter we are going to look at our true identity. This will be very important for understanding and enjoying the gospel in its fullness.

When (if) you accepted Christ as your Savior and put your faith in his work on the cross, the Bible teaches that you have been made a new creation. You have actually been *transformed* into your true identity; the identity that God created humans to be and have initially.

This is how God now sees you—a new creation. You're not just a saved sinner; you're in reality a restored, new creation in Christ.

Let's dive a little deeper into the implications of this.

STEP 2

A FEW CLARIFYING TRUTHS

CHAPTER 4

What You Do Does Not Equal Who You Are

Let me ask you a question. You'll have to be super honest about your answer if this is going to be helpful.

What voice in your head most defines you, right now?

Is it words from a teacher or parent?

Is it self-talk?

Many of us live day-to-day with a voice in our head that is reinforcing what we believe to be true of ourselves. It may be really negative or it could be really positive. It may be lies that the accuser (Satan) speaks to us daily in order to rob us of our joy and effectiveness in living out the truth of the Kingdom.

However, if it's not the Father's voice–if it's not what the Word of God and the Father tells us is true of us–then chances are it's self-made or someone else's-made, and it's not really true of you.

Another question:

Who or what gives you the most self-esteem or self-worth in your life?

Have you ever thought about that? Which person in your life (alive or not), or what activities, accomplishments, titles, or positions you hold gives you the most self-worth? Perhaps it's your pastor or maybe your mom or dad. It could be a teacher or coach that meant a lot to you.

If you derive your self worth from activity–what you *do*–it may be your parenting, or your job, title or degrees listed after your name. All of these different things make up our identity: how we perceive ourselves and believe (hope) others do as well.

But, what if your self-esteem and your identity was based *primarily* on being created in the image of God? (We'll go much farther into this in the next chapter.)

Whoa! Created in the image of God.

That would change everything, because now it would not be up to you to maintain an image that you didn't create in the first place. The pressure is off, right? The way of the world is: we do things (perform, serve, work etc.) to have value in the eyes of our family, friends, parents, spouse, siblings, boss, pastor etc.

WHAT YOU DO DOES NOT EQUAL WHO YOU ARE

If we do a good enough job and are perceived as valuable, then people will want us around. We will be wanted. We often form our identity out of this activity

What we *do* has led to who we *be* (are). Or at least we think it has. There is a huge problem with this and it is terribly dangerous. This belief will eventually crush us and it goes against how God now sees us.

Don't believe the
DO=BE
lies anymore.

Your actions do not define who you are. God defines you, your value and identity.

What you *do* does not equal who you *are*.

Sure, there are consequences for actions, both good and bad, but in Christ all sins have been paid for at the Cross and our actions don't define who we are. We are defined by God and by our original image-bearing that's now being restored in and through the work of Christ and the Holy Spirit in our lives. So your actions don't define who you are, nor does your past define your identity.

God doesn't see you as the person who used to do this or that. Like, *"That's my daughter and I saved her from a bunch of bad stuff and choices... But she doesn't do that anymore. Isn't that great?"*

The Bible says that in Christ, all sin has been forgiven and put away as far as the East is from the West. God chooses not to even remember it. So God doesn't look at us as the person who *used* to do anything. He looks at us as his dearly loved sons and daughters. That's how he sees you.

NEW EYES

Unfortunately, we often don't treat others that way. We see people as sort of the list of their accomplishments or a list of their failures and disappointments. Even though we might love them and tolerate all of their "stuff", we kind of keep it on the list, right? All of those things go on their "performance chart".

Not God. Not at all.

When the Christian faith becomes defined by what we do and not by who Christ is and what he did for us, we miss the gospel - and we, ironically, become more disobedient.
~Tullian Tchividjian

Our past doesn't define our identity. God does. Who Jesus is and what he accomplished on our behalf does. Your roles and your performance do not. Jesus already performed in the ultimate way when he died on the Cross to take the penalty for our sins and then rose again. Jesus is giving us new life and sharing his inheritance and all His authority with us.

Your roles don't define you, nor does your performance. So it doesn't matter if you have no title or the biggest title or all kinds

WHAT YOU DO DOES NOT EQUAL WHO YOU ARE

of degrees after your name. Whatever. It doesn't matter; none of that defines you. God sees you as his image-bearer and he sees you now in Christ and you have *his* righteousness.

That is huge.

This is part of a bigger gospel.

The more we understand and believe our true identity, and that it comes from God himself, the more freedom we will live with.

And we will be a living example of the good news of the gospel.

Buckle up. This is going to be quite a ride.

CHAPTER 5

Birthright: Your True Identity in Christ

So many of us have believed a tiny, truncated gospel. It is primarily about sin management, behavioral modification and someday getting out of here and going to heaven. But looking at the full story of God, and the bigger gospel found throughout all of scripture, we see this:

> You were created in the image of a loving and gracious God, and destined for an eternal relationship with him.

> Though it is true that you have rebelled against God, thinking you could create an identity for yourself, one where you are lord over your own life, God himself came on a rescue mission to restore

all people, places, and things back to relationship with him (including you), back to the way he originally designed it to be.

There is a day coming when he will once again walk and live and dwell with us in a city that is like a beautiful garden forever and ever.

It is out of the fuller story that we understand why we were created, understand God's plans for this world, and come to know our original—and now restored—identity.

Because we have God as our loving Father, we are dearly loved sons and daughters. We are a family. We are called to live as a family that has been sent and empowered by Jesus' own Spirit as missionaries, serving others as we have been served. A way of life. We don't do this because we are supposed to, but because this is who we are. We get to extend God's loving rescue mission to the ends of the earth.

We truly are a family of missionary servants sent as disciples who make disciples.

Now this is big. It has great implications for our lives. This is our birthright and our new, true identity in Christ. The more we believe this, the more we will live in freedom and live in light of who God says we are.

BIRTHRIGHT: YOUR TRUE IDENTITY IN CHRIST

A BILLION DOLLARS

Here's an illustration that will help you understand just how valuable all of this is. Your new identity in Christ is true of you even if you never heard this before or fully understood it. And like I've already said, it is your birthright.

Imagine that when you were born you had a great uncle who was very, very wealthy. He put a billion dollars into an annuity, into a bank account for you when you were a baby, okay? It was gonna grow and grow and grow so that when you were eighteen or maybe twenty-five years old, you would be able to take this money out. It would have grown *really* large by then.

But here's the problem. After your uncle puts this billion-dollar annuity in the bank for you, he's leaving the bank and he dies in a fiery car crash. No one knows that he did it. The bank does, but they're not expecting to hear anything for twenty-five years and all the proof of the account and the deposit slip is burned up. No one knows.

So you've lived your whole life not knowing what's true of you– that you are rich!

Then, let's say you're getting older, nearing retirement age or so. The kids are pretty much grown and now, because everything is digital, the bank finally gets a hold of you and they say, *"Hey, we've got some crazy news..."*. And it's awesome. They tell you the story and basically the gist of it is that you are freaky, super wealthy.

You're like, *"Oh my gosh!"* You are so excited, but you're also a little bit flabbergasted. Your life starts to flash before your eyes. You think of all the times that you weren't that generous or when you were stressing out about money or paying the mortgage. The times when you saw there was need (you know, someone in your family, your neighborhood or community) and you didn't meet it, because, well, you were saving for a vacation or whatever.

You think to yourself, *"I would have lived so differently if only I had known what was true of me. I'd have lived a completely different life if I'd known what was mine since birth and what had always been true of me."*

And that's what your true identity is like. This identity as a member of God's family of missionary servants is *your* birthright. You get to live out of it and it's huge. It's worth way more than a billion dollar annuity.

Please believe this is true of you now. It's not something you have to wait until heaven to inherit.

MOVING IT TO THE HEART

Here are a couple questions to help you take all of this and really seed it in your heart.

Q: What changes when you think of yourself as a dearly loved child in the family of God?

Q: How do you want to live with others? How do you want to treat others and be treated?

BIRTHRIGHT: YOUR TRUE IDENTITY IN CHRIST

Missionaries aren't just people who go to foreign lands. Scripture teaches that in Christ you are a missionary and that this is an identity thing.

Q: What would change in your life if you believe you are a full-time missionary?

Jesus is the King of Kings and he came as a missionary servant and laid his life down for you.

Q: How does Jesus' life motivate you to live as a servant to others?

Here again, we are not serving because we are supposed to, or because it makes us look good or it needs to get done. We get to serve because we have been so deeply served. Take some time with these questions. Let your transformed identity and the implications of this pump through your system a bit more.

Make a place at the table.

Go. Cross the fence, cross the street, cross the globe.

Die to something so that others may live.

Bounce your last check in generosity.

You get to! It's your birthright.

Now that we've clarified what is true of us, and how God now sees us, let's look at some life changing truths about God himself.

CHAPTER 6

Four Life-Changing Truths About God

If we are now new creations, where does sin come from? Why do we still sin even after we have acknowledged something as sin, and perhaps, repented of it over and over?

> *"Sinful acts always have their origin in some form of unbelief–behind every sin is a lie. The root of all our behavior and emotions is the heart, what it trusts and what it treasures. People are given over to sinful desires because 'they exchanged the truth of God for a lie'"*

My friend and author Tim Chester shared this with a group of us and it forever changed my view of sin.

The Bible puts it in similar terms:

They exchanged the truth about God for a lie...

Romans 1:25

Everything that does not come from faith is sin.

Romans 14:23

Another word for faith is belief, and these verses suggest that all sin comes from not believing what is true about God. Typically people want to blame their sin on their circumstances...*I got angry because the guy cut me off in traffic...I started to worry all the time because my husband lost his job...I yelled at the kids because they weren't obeying me...*But the reality is that our circumstances merely reveal what is already in our hearts.

Our struggles reveal our hearts.

This heart level perspective is a radical view of sin and repentance. But this perspective is also a very helpful view of sanctification and transformation because it very clearly shows us the way out. Most of us think that the way to stop sinning is to change our behavior. However, if behind every sin is a lie about God, then what really needs to change is what I am believing in my heart.

FOUR LIFE-CHANGING TRUTHS ABOUT GOD

THE 4 G'S

Here are four life-changing truths about God, that when not fully believed, lead to every human sin[7]:

God is Great
God is Glorious
God is Good
God is Gracious

Ok, you're thinking, *"I already believe these truths..."*, but if you are anything like me, when I first heard or read these "4 G's" I was at once drawn to one or two of these in my soul. The Spirit immediately convicted me that I had unbelief in some of these areas. There is much more that could be said about God than is covered by these four truths, but they give us a powerful diagnostic tool for addressing most of the sins and negative emotions that we struggle with.

Stress, fears, performance issues, ungratefulness, dishonesty, striving...

Notice that all of these are heart issues. There is *always* a heart issue behind every sinful action.

WHAT DOES IT MEAN TO "BELIEVE"?

According to the Bible, our hearts are far more than just a muscle in our chests pumping blood throughout our bodies. The word "heart" occurs over 850 times in the Bible. Our heart...makes decisions, it feels emotions, it can be deceived, it desires things, it lusts, it thinks and reasons.

The word "heart" is the word the Bible uses to describe the real you, the very center of your being. The heart includes your mind, emotions, and will. It is not less than any one of those things; it is more.

> *If you confess with your mouth, 'Jesus is Lord,' and believe in your heart that God raised him from the dead, you will be saved. **For it is with your heart that you believe and are justified**, and it is with your mouth that you confess and are saved.*
> Romans 10:9-10

Do you believe with your head? No. Ultimately you believe in your heart, the deepest part of who you are; your mind, your emotions and your will.

UNBELIEVERS... ALL OF US!

Not many Christians think of themselves as unbelievers. We normally use the term to describe people who are sojourners and not yet disciples of Jesus. But there are many things about God that we actually do not believe. Often there is a large gap between what we say we believe in our head, and what we truly believe in our heart.

I call this our Head–Heart Distortion.

The process of closing the gap between what we know in our head and what we believe in our heart is called sanctification. Sanctification is about becoming more like Jesus, but we will only become more like Jesus when our actions are consistent with what we say we believe.

Where in your experience have you believed one thing in your head, but acted out of a different heart motive, belief or perception?

THE TRUTH SHALL SET YOU FREE

Let's take a closer, deeper look at the lies we believe, some of the evidence that this is true, and how the truth about God can set us free from sin in each of these areas.

Growing in this perspective will be a big part of our gospel-fluency.

GOD IS GREAT...SO I DON'T HAVE TO BE IN CONTROL

We may know (and even say we believe) that God is in control of all things - that he is sovereign. Then we are filled with worry and anxiety about many of the details of our lives. It's as if we're saying, "I know in my head that God is in control, but I don't really believe in my heart that God is in control...or maybe he needs my help. Therefore, I must work to control certain people or situations in my life."

Ouch.

But if I truly believe that God is great, that he is large and in charge of EVERYTHING in life, then I can rest. I can repent of stressing out over people, circumstances or my future.

GOD IS GLORIOUS...SO I DON'T HAVE TO FEAR OTHERS

One common reason we sin is that we crave the approval of others or fear their rejection or disapproval. We 'need' the acceptance of a parent, boss, friend, spouse etc. so we are controlled by them and their opinion of us. The Bible's term for this is 'fear of man'.

> *Fear of man will prove to be a snare, but whoever trusts in the Lord is kept safe.*
> *Proverbs 29:25*

The answer to fear of man is fear of God. We need a bigger, better and more glorious view of God. The word glory means "weighty," as in "a person of importance, a weighty person." God should be the "weightiest" person in our lives.

GOD IS GOOD...SO I DON'T HAVE TO LOOK ELSEWHERE FOR MY SATISFACTION

God created humanity "needy". He gives us continual reminders of our need for him and his ongoing provision: hunger, thirst, exhaustion, and our quest for love, relationship and intimacy. None of these can be fulfilled from within ourselves. We were designed to need God.

When we look for fulfillment and satisfaction for these needs elsewhere in life, we become bitter and complaining. People and things will all eventually fail to satisfy. They cannot fill our souls deeply–the way we were created to experience. Instead of seeking ultimate satisfaction from food, drink, exercise, sleep, sex, or relationships, we need to trust the only One who can truly satisfy our needy hearts.

Jesus came to satisfy the hunger of our souls, to give us rest, to live in an intimate and loving relationship with us. Jesus is the better fulfillment for our every need.

GOD IS GRACIOUS…SO I DON'T HAVE TO PROVE MYSELF

We can spend our life trying to prove ourselves worthy, valuable or right. I want to prove to *myself* that I am good enough or desirable. I strive to impress *others* and constantly seek their validation and approval. Ultimately, we try to live in ways that God will be impressed with so that he will bless us or be happy with us.

The grace of God is so simple to understand and yet so hard to grasp. We seem to be hard-wired to think we must do something to make God look and act favorably towards us. Yet while we were still sinners, he sent his son Jesus to die in our place–the ultimate act of his grace toward us.

When we believe in our hearts that God is gracious, we will stop trying to prove ourselves and earn his love. We can truly *be* before him.

IDOL CHECK

Growing up in the church, whenever I heard the word idol or idolatry I thought of little stone statues or totem poles.

No problem with those in my life…check!

But idols are anything or anyone in our life that we put above God, in any way. We "serve" idols that give us the feelings or status we long for. Our hearts are idol factories; we hardly go a moment without placing our hope or trust in something or someone other than Jesus to fulfill us or make us whole.

When we learn to identify the idols of the heart that seek to control us, and speak gospel truth into those dark and destructive beliefs and desires, we are set free. Ultimately, Jesus is the greater, the more glorious, the better and most gracious one who crushes the idols of our heart.

Take a look at Appendix B to see how our idols are put to death by the 4 Gs.

Our Lord Jesus is the ultimate demonstration of what God is like. In his life, death and resurrection we see God's greatness, glory, goodness and grace most wonderfully and eternally put on display.

Now it's time to put this all together. Who God is, what he has done, and what is now true of us all forms the foundation for this process of applying the gospel to all of life.

STEP 3

A PROCESS FOR GROWING IN GOSPEL FLUENCY

CHAPTER ⟨ 7 ⟩

How the Gospel Speaks Into All of Life

I thought Becs was either going to hit the ceiling or hit Liesel in the head with the pan she was drying off. We had just had a nice dinner with these two friends who were visiting from England. The ladies had volunteered to help with washing up in our old dishwasher-less kitchen, when Liesel said something to Becs that blew me away. They were talking about some frustration that Becs was having with an employee at work and how frustrated she was that this other person was not going along with the program.

And that's when it happened.

I heard Liesel casually say to Becs, *"Hmmm, it seems that maybe your pride is being hurt. And what you're really upset about is that this person is not responding to you like you are God. Only God is great, sister, you don't have to be in control. Jesus died so you wouldn't have to be, you're free."*

Becs responded with, *"I do believe you're right. I don't like it when my sovereignty is thwarted… as if I am God over everyone else's choices. I need to repent of that. Thanks, sister!"*

And off they went, finishing up the dishes and chatting away as if nothing big had happened. I stood there wondering how often they had "gospeled" each other's hearts like this. Over time I came to realize that this is exactly what a gospel-centered community does. That's how discipleship happens—in the flow of everyday life and activity.

Even while you are washing up the dishes[8].

So how did my British sisters so quickly get to the truth of a potentially prickly issue? And in a way that was both delivered in normal conversation and received as really good news by Becs? By learning to ask, answer and apply very powerful questions to illuminate what's going on in our life or heart, and how the Gospel speaks into it.

When we are feeling or acting a certain way, in any situation, we can begin to understand how the Gospel speaks into it by asking and applying the same four questions:

1. Who is God?
2. What has He done?
3. What is now true of us?
4. How do we get to respond?

HOW THE GOSPEL SPEAKS INTO ALL LIFE

So, let's work this out. Let me take the 4 Questions and help you apply them to the issue of stress over money, or maybe, living with a lack of generosity. Perhaps the two are connected.

If that was the issue you were trying to address in your own heart, or in someone else that you're having a conversation with, here's how those four questions might be asked, answered and applied.

QUESTION #1: WHO IS GOD?

Answer: Look for his character qualities and attributes i.e. Father, faithful, patient, provider, etc.

While there could be a long list of truths about God connected to that issue, we could say, well, He's a good Father who owns it all. The Bible says, "he owns the cattle on a thousand hills". He created everything and it's all his. He's also super generous!

Let's move on the Question #2 which we will look at from three angles. What has He done to prove all of the above to us?

QUESTION #2: WHAT HAS HE DONE?

Answer: Look for his actions (i.e. how has God proven these character qualities to be true of himself in the past).

- **In the Bible:** *He provided for Adam and Eve even after they sinned. He gave Israel manna and water and food as they needed. God provided his own Son on the cross.*

Right from the beginning of the Story found in the Bible, God provides every need for Adam and Eve. Even after they sinned he clothed them in animal skins. He gave Israel manna, food and water, each time they had need–even though they were rebellious complainers.

And here's a biggie: God provided his own Son. Our greatest need was provided for in Jesus on the Cross.

I would say that is pretty super generous proof!

- **In your own life in the past:** *He provided for my family's needs after I was laid off. He moved someone to anonymously buy us a new refrigerator - ours had died!*

Has God ever provided for you in ways that you go, "Whoa!"? He can and often does show up with great generosity in surprising ways. Remembering the ways he has provided for you in the past will help you trust in his provision for your future.

- **Through the life, death and resurrection of Jesus:** *Jesus willingly gave his life in place of mine–the ultimate provision! He gave us his Spirit.*

This is where the gospel rubber really meets the road. Jesus willingly gave his life in place of ours. He is the ultimate provision, the ultimate in generosity. And he also gave us his own Spirit to protect and guide us through every situation in life.

That is crazy generous!

Then, in light of all of that, we want to ask the third question. Based on what is true of God and what he has done to prove it, what is now true of us in connection with this topic of stress over money and generosity?

QUESTION #3: WHAT IS NOW TRUE OF US?

Answer: This is all connected to what the Bible teaches is true of your identity, authority and privilege (i.e. dearly loved sons and daughters, fully accepted, part of a big family, missionary, servant etc).

In Christ we *are* dearly loved sons and daughters. We're well provided for. Daddy owns it all and he loves us, He's not going to hang us out there to dry. We're co-heirs with Christ. Amazing. And we're part of God's BIG family.

God is routing his endless resources, in his timing, through all kinds of people to get it to us.

We can believe it. This is now true of us.

QUESTION #4: HOW DO WE GET TO RESPOND?

Answer: What will your actions or emotions be in light of who God is, what he has done, and what is true of you? How will you now live or act?)

We can trust God for our financial needs, even those that are unforeseen. We can be generous and live generously in giving and meeting other's needs.

Knowing that even if we feel like we have lack, our heavenly Dad doesn't lack, so we can be generous. We don't have to stress. He has what we need.

Living this way will be a huge witness to others. It's powerful stuff.

> *The gospel alone liberates you to live a life of scandalous generosity, unrestrained sacrifice, uncommon valor, and unbounded courage.*
> *~Tullian Tchividjian*

ONE MORE TIME, RIGHT IN A ROW, FOR CLARITY

So that I can be sure that you are seeing how all of this fits together, let me risk being overly redundant (you like that?) and show you what this looks like laid out in a bulleted list:

The 4 Questions: Applied to stress over money or lack of generosity

1. Who is God? *A good father who owns it all and is super-generous to us.*

2. What has He done? *(We look in three areas:)*

- **In the Bible:** *He provided for Adam and Eve even after they sinned. He gave Israel manna and water and food as they needed. God provided his own Son on the cross.*

- **In your own life in the past:** *He provided for my family's needs after I was laid off. He moved someone to anonymously buy us a new refrigerator-ours had died!*

- **Through the life, death and resurrection of Jesus:** *Jesus willingly gave his life in place of mine-the ultimate provision! He gave us his Spirit.*

3. What is now true of us? *Identity stuff: dearly loved sons and daughters, well provided for, co-heirs with Christ, part of a big Family*

4. How do we get to respond? *We can be generous in giving and meeting other's needs, we can trust God for our finances and needs-even those that are unforeseen. (A HUGE witness to others!)*

That is one example of how the 4 questions can help lead us to the truth of the Gospel and lead us out of stress over money or lack of generosity in our lives. It is by remembering and rehearsing the ways he has provided for you in the past that you learn to trust in His provision for your future.

This can be applied to *any* situation–either negative or positive. These four questions will lead us to focus on God and his greatness (instead of our lack) and will then lead us to respond in freedom. And you may have noticed; the use of the 4 Gs we learned in Chapter 6 are a great place to start when looking for the unbelief behind any given attitude or action.

GET MY WORKSHEET

I will send you a worksheet you can use to walk through these four questions, along with another example of what this looks like if you go to: **caesarkalinowski.com/4questions**

There are unlimited conversations that can and will happen in your life. I'll give you another good case study if you hit me up at the link above. It will add further clarity for you.

Check out Appendix A in the back of this book for a list of attributes and character traits of God and a long list of what is now true of us because of the gospel.

Check out Appendix C to see how some folks in my tribe ask and answer the question, "What is God saying and how will I respond to it?" using what is called the *Kairos Circle* which we also employ the 4 Questions.

Now let's look at how we can use these same four questions in reverse order to lead us from unbelief to belief in any area of life.

CHAPTER 8

Turn This Around:
It Works in Reverse Too

"She just flipped out when I said _I can't come_."

"I just flipped out when my kids _didn't_ listen."

"I am really depressed and anxious about _life_ right now."

"The way he acted about _me_ was just plain sinful."

"The words I said when _angry_ happened were sinful."

You can fill in the blanks of your own last sinful action or encounter with someone else. But whatever it was that was said or done in sin has unbelief at its core. Unbelief is always the "thing behind the thing" when it comes to sin. And that unbelief needs to be uncovered, addressed and repented of in order to move forward.

The 4 Questions work in these situations brilliantly. We will just need to flip the order around so we move from "How did I/they respond?" toward "Who is God and what is he like?"

BUT YOU SAID YOU WOULD DO IT!

Remember a time when you were angry with a friend or your spouse for not following through on a chore or something they said they would do. You may still be angry. Maybe that's happening in your life right now. Can you imagine it? There's probably been a time when that was how you responded; in anger and self-righteousness.

Now let's try asking and applying the same 4 Questions in reverse order to see how the Gospel speaks into this situation. It's amazing.

QUESTION #4: HOW DID WE RESPOND?

Answer: *We are/were angry with a friend or spouse for not following through on a chore / something they said they'd do.*

So, that's how we responded. Not the best, right? There's a good chance that this response is keeping your relationship in a place that is not its best.

Now, let's ask ourselves Question #3, "what is true of us?

QUESTION #3: WHAT IS TRUE OF US?

Answer: *We're children of a sovereign Father who **alone** controls people and this world. His care is in place for us regardless of* *others performance. He's working all things together for our good and His glory.*

Okay, this is sounding like good news already.

We're children of a loving and sovereign Father, who alone controls all things. We do not. His care and favor is in place for us regardless of others' performance or our own. I am glad of that! He is working all things together for our good and, this is important: His glory.

That's true for us.

God is Sovereign and we're not.

Can you see how that speaks the gospel into us being angry over other people's actions, or inactions? If God is sovereign and knows these things, is there anything to be angry about?

Let's move on the Question #2 which we will look at from three angles. Of course there could be many more answers to each, but you'll get the idea.

QUESTION #2: WHAT HAS HE DONE?

- **In the Bible:** *David was a mighty king who could not control his own actions or those of his own children or troops, yet God worked out his care and gained Himself glory.*

If you don't know the story of David, you might want to go read it. He was a mighty King, but he was also a great sinner and he couldn't control his own actions at times or his children or his troops... and yet God blessed him and cared for him in powerful ways.

That shows us something beautiful about God and his heart and character.

- **In your own life in the past:** *At times I have not followed through on things I promised I would do, or promises made to God, and He still cared for me and loved me through the consequences.*

Wow! That's powerful. That begins to soften my heart in light of what he's done. It also further shifts the focus to him and my worship (worth-ship) of him.

And now let's look at what was accomplished on our behalf...

- **Through the life, death and resurrection of Jesus:** *I made a mess of much of my life due to my poor decisions and thinking I "got this" and Jesus pursued me and paid the penalty for all of my "poor choices" (i.e. sin)!*

Ultimately, this is the big one. It always is. I made a mess of much of my life due to my poor decisions and belief that I am god and in control of things. Like I'm king of my universe, king of the world here. Still, Jesus pursued me and pursued me. He was patient and he pursued me.

Redundant, I know... But I need that!

TURN THIS AROUND: IT WORKS IN REVERSE TOO

Even when I was performing horribly (living in sin), he willingly paid the penalty for all my poor choices and "bad" performance.

That changes things. That changes *me*.

Can you see how the focus is now shifting away from what *we did* to what God *has done* and how amazing he is instead of how sinful we are?!

That leads us to Question #1. We're still going back in the other direction here. This is where we really start to shift from unbelief to belief in what is, and will always be, true of God. This is what we need to get to every time.

QUESTION #1: WHO IS GOD?

Answer: *A good father who alone is sovereign! (I am not). A savior who has taken all stress and sin upon himself (I can't do that). And he did this when I did not obey him or follow his ways…He blessed me and was patient despite my performance.*

There is so much that correlates here when we ask, "Who is God?" Please always feel free to write down your answers to all 4 Questions in as much detail as you can.

In light of this situation, who is God? He's a good father, who alone is sovereign.

He (Jesus) is a savior who has taken all stress and sin upon himself. I can't do that. He did this, even when I did not obey him or follow his ways perfectly. Which is pretty much all of the time.

God has blessed me and he is patient, despite my performance.

So that leads me to think, "Well, I can respond differently now. I don't have to be stressed. I don't have to be angry with others who don't submit to my 'sovereignty'"

By the way, this is what's really going on when we get upset with someone. When we get impatient or angry or stressed out over situations, we are believing that our sovereignty is being thwarted. People aren't treating us like we are God and large and in charge.

In light of what is true of God, so therefore true of me, I now *get to* choose a different response to the situation. A gospel-fluent response.

I am humbled and God looks amazing!

The way it should be.

ONE MORE TIME, RIGHT IN A ROW, FOR CLARITY

Question #4: How did we respond? *We are/were angry with our friend or spouse for not following through on a chore / something they said they'd do.*

Question #3: What is true of us? *We're children of a sovereign Father who **alone** controls people and this world. His care is in place for us regardless of others performance (or our own). He's working all things together for our good and His glory.*

TURN THIS AROUND: IT WORKS IN REVERSE TOO

Question #2: What has He done? *(we look in three areas:)*

- **In the Bible:** *David was a mighty king who could not control his own actions or those of his own children or troops, yet God worked out his care and gained Himself glory!*

- **In your own life in the past:** *At times I have not followed through on things I promised I would do, or promises made to God and He still cared for me and loved me through the consequences.*

- **Through the life, death and resurrection of Jesus:** *I made a mess of much of my life due to my poor decisions and thinking I "got this" and still Jesus pursued me and paid the penalty for all of my "poor choices" (sin)!*

Question #1: Who is God? *A good Father who alone is sovereign! (I am not). A Savior who has taken all stress and sin upon himself (I can't do that). He did this when I did not obey Him or follow His ways. He blessed me and was patient with me despite my performance.*

Hopefully, you can now see how these 4 Questions asked in reverse help us work our way back out of a sinful attitude, situation or habit. This of course works the same when helping others move from unbelief to belief as well.

In these situations you'll need to go slowly, gently as you bring the good news.

You'll need to practice this, just like any other "new language".

But I am confident if you will, trusting the Holy Spirit to guide you, you'll soon be using these 4 Questions and experiencing the gospel in more and more areas of life.

Sometimes, even when we have new tools and insight, old patterns of fear or self-protection can keep us from finding freedom or setting others free.

It's time to come out into the light.

Your world is waiting.

CHAPTER 9

Let Your Redemption Show
Lose the Fear of Rejection

Adam and Eve having their first argument after leaving the Garden:

Adam: *I'm getting pretty hungry, what's for dinner?*

Eve: *There's not much...do you want a piece of fruit to hold you over 'til dinner?*

Adam: *Um, I think I'll pass. That didn't work out so well for us last time.*

Eve: *What are you saying? What are you getting at Adam? Are you saying that it's my fault we're out here?!*

Adam: *All I know is that I left you alone for a second, talking to a walking, talking serpent, and the next thing I know...*

Eve: *It's like you think you're perfect or something!*

Adam: *I was!*

WE AND US AND I

Scripture and virtually all of history have shown us that if there is one thing we have most in common with every other human being, it's our sinful nature. *No one* is perfect, not by a long shot. Yet, usually we let other's sins define them—and divide us—when in fact we are all sinners in need of the same Savior. We're all dying, literally, and in need of rescue.

We're just alike[9].

So let your redemption show. Don't hide the forgiveness and changes that you're experiencing in Christ.

When we can be honest about where we're at in our own lives, and our own spiritual need, it also gives others the permission to do the same. Something shifts—in our hearts and in our interactions with others. If we stop pretending that we have all the answers and that our lives are perfect, we can also drop the need to win the argument, fix everyone or close the deal on their salvation. Ask yourself if others feel safe to approach you, even with their sins and screw-ups?

The pressure is off!

For you.

For them.

And by the way, I'm talking about with other believers too, not just with non-Christians.

THIS ONE THING REMAINS

Regardless of your methods and motives, or how fluent in the gospel you are becoming, one thing remains: many people *still* don't share their faith or speak the truth in love within their family and community because of the fear of rejection.

FEAR OF REJECTION SOUNDS LIKE THIS:

- I feel awkward and uncomfortable talking about my faith with others.

- I tried in the past and it never ended well.

- I can remember friends trying to "jam their religion down my throat" before I became a Christian and I vowed never to be that way.

- I'm worried that I might ruin my friendships if I bring up Jesus or spiritual things.

- No one likes to be "fixed" by another Christian

- If I admit that I am not perfect, they may think less of me.

- I fear rejection so much that I cannot risk it.

If you're like me you can relate to at least a few of these. And maybe you have other reasons of your own. But now that you're learning the language of the gospel it doesn't have to stay that way.

WHY WE FEAR REJECTION

Love of self.
The biggest reason we fear rejection is that we really love ourselves and we love to be liked. This may be hard to hear, but the main thing that is responsible for closing our mouths when it comes to the gospel is a love of self. We are afraid to lose the approval of those around us. We love ourselves more than we love others, Jesus and his glory.

We think we have to "close the sale."
I can remember being taught how to take any conversation and transition it into a sales pitch for Jesus and maneuver the listener towards saying the "Jesus in my heart prayer" right there on the spot. I hated feeling like a salesman and almost always avoided this. I am pretty sure my friends hated it more.

I never know when it's the right time.
Just because we can see another person's sin or pain in their life, and we know the gospel and how Jesus can bring healing to them, it doesn't mean that *right now* is the time to discuss it. Proverbs 25:11 teaches that a word spoken in the right circumstances is like apples of gold in settings of silver. One translation says, "a word in season...".

We don't know what to say.
Many of us have spent years listening to sermons, studying theology and reading the Bible, but still feel intimidated or unable to naturally express the good news of the gospel into normal life, conversations, and circumstances. This should become less and less an issue for you now. Remember, your new gospel fluency will grow and become even *better* news as you use it. Start with yourself and your family and let it grow outwards, naturally.

Apparently, there are better times than others to "share the good news" or witness or apply the gospel. Even done with gentleness and good gospel fluency, now may not be the best time. Ask the Spirit to guide you in these situations. God knows the *perfect* time (and words) and is preparing both of your hearts in his will. You can trust him for this.

Now let me give you three insights that have helped me move past the fear of rejection.

Beat the Fear of Rejection

Remember that you are already perfectly loved by God.
Because we have the love of a wonderful Father in heaven, we can move away from our deep-rooted fear of what others think of us. God loves us just the same if we ever share our faith or not.

Because we don't have to perform to gain his love and acceptance, we are freed from feeling like we have to perform for others as well. Let God's perfect love replace your own imperfect love of self.

Our huffing and puffing to impress God, our scrambling for brownie points, our thrashing about trying to fix ourselves while hiding our pettiness and wallowing in guilt are nauseating to God and are a flat out denial of the gospel of grace.
                                                            ~Brennan Manning

Take a longer view of evangelism.
My good friend Hugh Halter says that when he becomes friends with a not-yet believer, he plans on it taking around 5 years for them to see and hear enough about Jesus and his Kingdom to come to faith in him.

All of life—every conversation, times together, happy and sad moments are all filled with opportunity to both display and proclaim the gospel. Jesus said we are to be a "friend of sinners" (like he was). But he did not say to be their friend so *that* you can close the deal and get them saved.

Faith and salvation are gifts from God. That's his business and timing.

Continue to grow in gospel fluency.
The thing that has made the biggest difference when it comes to naturally sharing my faith with others, or living out the gospel with other believers, is growing in my gospel fluency.

You're on that path now! Instead of having to wait for an "in", or roll out a canned presentation, you're learning how to relationally speak about Jesus, your faith and the gospel wherever you are, in any situation.

If you love well, focus on other's needs, and continue to grow in your gospel fluency, over time you'll look back and realize that you have shared your faith with friends so many times over, that your life–including your words–has been one big testimony.

THE JOURNEY CONTINUES

At this point of the journey you have begun the real quest: to know and believe a Bigger Gospel and apply it to your life and others'.

This is at the very center of discipleship.

The gospel is not the beginning of the journey as a Christian; it is good news for *all* of life!

WHAT'S NEXT?

RESOURCES FOR YOUR JOURNEY INTO GOSPEL FLUENCY

WHAT'S NEXT?

You've done quite a bit of heavy lifting in the last few chapters of this book. And really, you're just at the beginning. Unlike me, and my caveman sounding utterances of the Czech language, I want to see you grow in your gospel fluency by leaps and bounds. Learning to *speak*, live and enjoy the Good News in every area of life takes practice. It's all there—it's all truth already—but we don't always see and experience it. Now you can.

We started out by asking a few clarifying questions. We looked briefly at the traditional evangelism and discipleship continuum. Understanding the distinction and pattern that Jesus gave us changes everything.

WHAT'SNEXT?

Next we looked at the historical use of apologetics and discovered that it is in fact not a dirty word—or practice—if used properly.

Wrapping up Part 1 we asked and answered, "What is the Gospel?" This is perhaps the most important question we could ask and bring clarity too. From this we discovered and experienced a much *Bigger Gospel*.

In Part 2 you were given a few clarifying truths about your true identity and birthright in Christ. Do you believe this is true of you? Please stop believing the DO=BE lies.

Powerful!

Finally, I shared those four eternal truths about God (the 4 Gs) that help us discover the lies about God that lurk behind all human sin. This is still one of the most useful tools in my gospel-fluency toolbox.

I hope you will re-visit and speak the 4 Gs to yourself and others every day! Check out Appendix B to look at common idols that our unbelief is fed by.

THE 4 QUESTIONS

From there, I unpacked for you the full process for seeing and applying the gospel to any and every situation in our lives. By now you should have a very detailed knowledge of how to use the 4 Questions applied to what God is saying to you or in light of sin in your life and the lives of others.

RESOURCES FOR YOUR JOURNEY INTO GOSPEL FLUENCY

And this doesn't just apply to sin. Any situation that someone finds himself or herself in can be re-centered in the truth and good news of the gospel; things like pain, loss, fear, anxiety, needs. There is good news in the gospel for all of these, and this same process will help you first think through and then speak the good news to people in each of them.

Using the 4 Questions will become second nature as you engage and share them with others in your life. Remember, I will send you a worksheet you can use to walk through these 4 Questions, along with another example of what this looks like, if you go to: caesarkalinowski.com/4questions

TAKE THIS FURTHER...YOU'RE READY

I also want to invite you to enroll in my short online course: **A Bigger Gospel – A Master Class in Gospel Fluency.**

In this video-driven course, I walk you through everything contained in this book. Together, I'll go step-by-step, giving you specific action steps, lot's of additional tools and a series of case studies where you can "listen in" on several people using their gospel fluency to address sin, tension or other unbelief in their lives.

Good news that actually sounds like good news!

Check out all of the details for this course at: **123lifeschool.com/bg-masterclass**

WHAT'S NEXT?

DO THIS IN COMMUNITY

Growing in gospel fluency and experiencing a bigger gospel is actually a team sport. Please don't attempt this in isolation. Just like with any other "language", it must be used, spoken and experienced together with others in order to shape and reshape culture. Starting with the culture in our homes and churches.

Going through a resource like *The Gospel Primer* in community will also super-charge your growth. You can find this tool at missiopublishing.com

Please share this book and what you are learning with others. I wish I could accurately convey how what I have shared here has changed my family, our church and countless leaders we work with around the world.

Bless others. Give out copies of this book as a gift to a friend, or your staff. Watch how this starts to soak into every conversation and illuminate the "thing behind the thing" in all of life.

This bigger gospel is worth giving our best time, passions and resources to. It's an investment that pays off in eternal dividends that you get to "cash in" now!I want to hear your story.

Write me at caesar@caesarkalinowski.com and tell me how you are beginning to live, speak and enjoy a bigger gospel.

I can't wait to hear from you!

Caesar Kalinowski

APPENDIX A

As you work through the process that you learned in Chapter 7 and 8, asking and applying the Four Questions, here is a partial list of attributes of God and some of what is now true of you. This will help you to grow in your ability to speak the good news into all of life.

WHAT IS TRUE OF GOD

Attributes and Qualities

Seeing and believing deeply that God is our true and loving Father is an important part of expressing the gospel to ourselves and to others.

APPENDIX A

We have the Father's never-ending love; we are his dearly loved sons and daughters.

"I will be a Father to you and you will be my sons and daughters, says the Lord

Almighty." (2 Corinthians 6:18 & 2 Samuel 7:14)

"For you did not receive a spirit that makes you a slave again to fear, but you received the Spirit of sonship. And by him we cry, `Abba, Father.'" (Romans 8:15)

"A Father to the fatherless, a defender of widows, is God in his holy dwelling. God sets the lonely in families, he leads forth the prisoners with singing." (Psalm 68:5-6)

"O Lord you are our Father. We are the clay, you are the potter; we are the work of your hands." (Isaiah 64:8)

"Your Father, who sees what is done in secret, will reward you." (Matthew 6:4)

"Your Father knows what you need before you ask him." (Matthew 6:8)

"Look at the birds of the air; they do not sow or reap or store away in barns, and yet your Heavenly Father feeds them. Are you not much more valuable than they?" (Matthew 6:26)

"If you then, though you are evil, know how to give good gifts to your children, how much more will your Father in heaven give good gifts to those who ask him!" (Matthew 7:11)

APPENDIX A

"Your Father in heaven is not willing that any one of these little ones should be lost." (Matthew 18:14)

"But while he was still a long way off, his father saw him and was filled with compassion for him; he ran to his son, threw his arms around him and kissed him... But the father said to his servants, `Quick! Bring the best robe and put it on him. Put a ring on his finger and sandals on his feet. Bring the fattened calf and kill it. Let's have a feast and celebrate. For this son of mine was dead and is alive again; he was lost and is found.'" (Luke 15:20b, 22-24)

"And I will ask the Father, and he will give you another Counselor [or Comforter] to be with you forever – the Spirit of Truth." (John 14:16)

"The Father will give you whatever you ask in [Jesus'] name." (John 15:16)

"Praise be to the God and Father of our Lord Jesus Christ, who has blessed us in the heavenly realms with every spiritual blessing in Christ. For he chose us.... In love he predestined us to be adopted as his [children]." (Ephesians 1:3-5)

"Through [Christ] we... have access to the Father by one Spirit." (Ephesians 2:18)

"[God is] the Father from whom all fatherhood derives its name." (Ephesians 3:15)

"Now to [the Father] who is able to do immeasurably more

than all we ask or imagine, according to his power that is at work within us, to him be glory in the church and in Christ Jesus throughout all generations, for ever and ever! Amen." (Ephesians 3:20-21)

"How great is the love the Father has lavished on us that we should be called children of God!" (1 John 3:1)

These Hebrew names of God are powerful and provide great insight into who God is and what he is like.

Adonai – *God is the Lord over all*
He is the King of kings and the Lord of lords, He reigns forever. Therefore you find safety in Him and Him alone. (Genesis 15:2, Psalm 2:4, 8:1, Isaiah 1:24)

Attiyq Youm – *The Ancient of Days*
God is eternal. He was before the beginning of time. Therefore He has all authority. Every knee bows before Him. (Daniel 7:9, 13, 14)

Elohim – *God is creator, powerful and mighty*
He is stronger and mightier than anyone or anything. When you face impossible circumstances or adversaries, now that your God is stronger. (Gen. 1:1, 17:7, Ps 19:1, Jer. 31:33)

El-Elyon – *The most high God*
Do not fear the enemy who tries to intimidate you. Know that your God is the Most High God. There is none above Him. Jesus Christ is exalted high above every name. (Genesis 14:17-20, Deuteronomy 26:19, Isaiah 14:13-14)

APPENDIX A

El-Gibhor – *Mighty God*
The Lord is mighty to save. His arm is not too short. Whatever problem you are facing, know that your God is MIGHTY! (Isaiah 9:6)

El-Olam – *The everlasting God*
God is eternal, while your problems are temporary. His love will never change. His promises are true. (Isaiah 40:28-31)

El-Roi – *The strong one who sees*
When you feel lonely and abandoned by people, know that God is with you. He sees you and He knows you. (Genesis 16:13)

El-Chuwl – *The God who gave birth*
God is our Creator and our Father. He saw us and He loved us, even before we were born. He has a plan for your life. (Psalm 139:13-18)

El-Deah – *God of knowledge*
Wisdom comes from the Lord. Man tries to become wise apart from God, but ends up in foolishness. (1 Samuel 2:3; Romans 11:33-36; 1 Cor. 1:18-31)

Yahweh – *The self-existent One*
He has always existed and will always exist. You can always rely on Him because He is your eternal source of strength. (Genesis 2:4, Isaiah 40:3; 10; 1)

Yahweh-Maccaddeshem – *The Lord your sanctifier*
He forgives your sins and His Holy Spirit works in your life to conform you to Himself: pure, loving and true. (Exodus 31:13, Leviticus 20:8; Ezekiel 37:28)

Yahweh-Rohi – *The Lord my shepherd*
He cares for you, the way a shepherd tends his sheep. He cares for you and leads you to still waters and green pastures. (Psalm 23, Isaiah 40:11)

Yahweh-Shammah – *The Lord who is present*
He never leaves you, nor forsakes you. He is with your forever who never betrays you. (Genesis 28:15, Psalm 23:4, 46:1, Jeremiah 23:23-24)

Yahweh-Rapha – *The Lord our healer*
Not only was God the healer in the Old Testament, but Jesus Christ revealed the healing heart of God for all of us, more than ever. Jesus Christ died to give you life. (Exodus 15:26, 2 Chronicles 7:14, Psalm 147:3, Jeremiah 17:14)

Yahweh-Tsidkenu – *The Lord our righteousness*
When we believe in Jesus Christ, He becomes our righteousness. He forgives our sins and washes us. (Jeremiah 23:6, Genesis 15:6, Psalm 4:1, 5:8, 24:5)

Yahweh-Jireh – *The Lord will provide*
Jesus Christ said that Father cares for us and we never need to worry about provision. He is our source of life, in every way. (Genesis 22:13-14)

Yahweh-Shalom – *The Lord is peace*
Whenever there are storms in your life, hide in Him. He is your shelter in the storm. He gives peace beyond understanding, even when circumstances are chaotic. (Judges 6:24)

APPENDIX A

Here are more attributes of God as expressed throughout scripture.

ABBA (Romans 8:15)
ADVOCATE (I John 2:1 kjv)
ALMIGHTY (Genesis 17:1)
ALL IN ALL (Colossians 3:11)
ALPHA (Revelation 22:13)
AMEN (Revelation 3:14)
ANOINTED ONE (Psalm 2:2)
APOSTLE (Hebrews 3:1)
ARM OF THE LORD (Isaiah 53:1)
AUTHOR OF ETERNAL SALVATION (Hebrews 5:9)
AUTHOR OF OUR FAITH (Hebrews 12:2)
AUTHOR OF PEACE (1 Cor. 14:33)
AVENGER (1 Thessalonians 4:6)

BEGINNING (Revelation 21:6)
BLESSED & HOLY RULER (1 Timothy 6:15)
BREAD OF LIFE (John 6:35)
BREATH OF LIFE (Genesis 2:7, Revelation 11:11)
BRIDEGROOM (Isaiah 62:5)
BRIGHT MORNING STAR (Revelation 22:16)

CAPTAIN OF SALVATION (Hebrews 2:10)
CHIEF SHEPHERD (1 Peter 5:4)
CHOSEN ONE (Isaiah 42:1)
CHRIST (Matthew 22:42)
CHRIST OF GOD (Luke 9:20)
CHRIST THE LORD (Luke 2:11)
COMFORTER (John 14:26 kjv)
COMMANDER (Isaiah 55:4)
CONSUMING FIRE (Deut. 4:24, Heb. 12:29)

APPENDIX A

CORNERSTONE (Isaiah 28:16)
COUNSELOR (Isaiah 9:6)
CREATOR (1 Peter 4:19)
CROWN OF BEAUTY (Isaiah 28:5)

DELIVERER (Romans 11:26)
DESIRED OF ALL NATIONS (Haggai 2:7)
DOOR (John 10:7 kjv)
DWELLING PLACE (Psalm 90:1)

ELECT ONE (Isaiah 42:1)
END (Revelation 21:6)
ETERNAL GOD (Deut. 33:27)
ETERNAL LIFE (1 John 5:20)
ETERNAL SPIRIT (Hebrews 9:14)
EVERLASTING FATHER (Isaiah 9:6)
EVERLASTING GOD (Genesis 21:33)
EXCELLENT (Psalm 148:13 kjv)

FAITHFUL & TRUE (Revelation 19:11)
FAITHFUL WITNESS (Revelation 1:5)
FATHER (Matthew 6:9)
FIRSTBORN (Rom.8:29, Rev.1:5, Col.1:15)
FIRSTFRUITS (1 Cor.15:20-23)
FORTRESS (Jeremiah 16:19)
FOUNDATION (1 Cor. 3:11)
FOUNTAIN OF LIVING WATERS (Jeremiah 2:13)
FRIEND (Matthew 11:19)
FULLERS' SOAP (Malachi 3:2 kjv)

GENTLE WHISPER (1 Kings 19:12)
GIFT OF GOD (John 4:10)
GLORY OF THE LORD (Isaiah 40:5)

APPENDIX A

GOD (Genesis 1:1)
GOD ALMIGHTY (Genesis 17:1)
GOD OF THE WHOLE EARTH (Isaiah 54:5)
GOD OVER ALL (Romans 9:5)
GOD WHO SEES ME (Genesis 16:13)
GOODNESS (Psalm 144:2 kjv)
GOOD SHEPHERD (John 10:11)
GOVERNOR (Psalm 22:28 kjv)
GREAT HIGH PRIEST (Hebrews 4:14)
GREAT SHEPHERD (Hebrews 13:20)
GUIDE (Psalm 48:14)

HEAD OF THE BODY (Colossians 1:18)
HEAD OF THE CHURCH (Ephesians 5:23)
HEIR OF ALL THINGS (Hebrews 1:2)
HIDING PLACE (Psalm 32:7)
HIGHEST (Luke 1:76)
HIGH PRIEST (Hebrews 3:1)
HIGH PRIEST FOREVER (Hebrews 6:20)
HOLY GHOST (John 14:26)
HOLY ONE (Acts 2:27)
HOLY ONE OF ISRAEL (Isaiah 49:7)
HOLY SPIRIT (John 15:26)
HOPE (Titus 2:13)
HORN OF SALVATION (Luke 1:69)
HUSBAND (Isaiah 54:5, Jer. 31:32, Hosea 2:16)

I AM (Exodus 3:14, John 8:58)
IMAGE OF GOD (2 Cor. 4:4)
IMAGE OF HIS PERSON (Hebrews 1:3)
IMMANUEL (Isaiah 7:14, Matthew 1:23)
INTERCESSOR (Romans 8:26,27,34 Hebrews 7:25)

APPENDIX A

JEALOUS (Exodus 34:14)
JESUS CHRIST OUR LORD (Romans 6:23)
JUDGE (Isaiah 33:22, Acts 10:42)
JUST ONE (Acts 22:14)

KEEPER (Psalm 121:5)
KING ETERNAL (1 Timothy 1:17)
KING OF GLORY (Psalm 24:10)
KING OF JEWS (Matthew 27:11)
KING OF KINGS (1 Timothy 6:15)
KING OF SAINTS (Revelation 15:3)

LAMB OF GOD (John 1:29)
LAST ADAM (1 Cor. 15:45)
LAWGIVER (Isaiah 33:22)
LEADER (Isaiah 55:4)
LIFE (John 14:6)
LIGHT OF THE WORLD (John 8:12)
LIKE AN EAGLE (Deut. 32:11)
LIVING GOD (Daniel 6:20)
LIVING STONE (1 Peter 2:4)
LIVING WATER (John 4:10)
LORD (John 13:13)
LORD GOD ALMIGHTY (Revelation 15:3)
LORD GOD OF HOSTS (Jeremiah 15:16)
LORD JESUS CHRIST (1 Cor. 15:57)
LORD OF ALL (Acts 10:36)
LORD OF GLORY (1 Cor. 2:8)
LORD OF HARVEST (Matthew 9:38)
LORD OF HOSTS (Haggai 1:5)
LORD OF LORDS (1 Tim. 6:15)
LORD OUR RIGHTEOUSNESS (Jeremiah 23:6)
LOVE (1 John 4:8)

APPENDIX A

LOVINGKINDNESS (Psalm 144:2)

MAKER (Job 35:10, Psalm 95:6)
MAJESTY ON HIGH (Hebrews 1:3)
MAN OF SORROWS (Isaiah 53:3)
MASTER (Luke 5:5)
MEDIATOR (1 Timothy 2:5)
MERCIFUL GOD (Jeremiah 3:12)
MESSENGER OF THE COVENANT (Malachi 3:1)
MESSIAH (John 4:25)
MIGHTY GOD (Isaiah 9:6)
MIGHTY ONE (Isaiah 60:16)
MOST UPRIGHT (Isaiah 26:7)

NAZARENE (Matthew 2:23)

OMEGA (Revelation 22:13)
ONLY BEGOTTEN SON (John 1:18 kjv)
OUR PASSOVER LAMB (1 Cor. 5:7)

PEACE (Ephesians 2:14)
PHYSICIAN (Luke 4:23)
PORTION (Psalm 73:26,Psalm 119:57)
POTTER (Isaiah 64:8)
POWER OF GOD (1 Cor. 1:24)
PRINCE OF LIFE (Acts 3:15)
PRINCE OF PEACE (Isaiah 9:6)
PROPHET (Acts 3:22)
PROPHET OF THE HIGHEST (Luke 1:76)
PROPITIATION (1John 2:2, 1John 4:10)
PURIFIER (Malachi 3:3)

RADIANCE OF GOD'S GLORY (Heb.1:3)

APPENDIX A

REDEEMER (Job 19:25)
REFINER'S FIRE (Malachi 3:2)
REFUGE (Jeremiah 16:19)
RESURRECTION (John 11:25)
REWARDER (Hebrews 11:6)
RIGHTEOUS ONE (1 John 2:1)
ROCK (1 Cor.10:4)
ROOT OF DAVID (Rev. 22:16)
RULER OF GOD'S CREATION (Rev. 3:14)
RULER OVER KINGS OF EARTH (Rev 1:5)

SAVIOR (Luke 2:11)
SEED (Genesis 3:15)
SERVANT (Isaiah 42:1)
SHADE (Psalm 121:5)
SHEPHERD OF OUR SOULS (1Peter 2:25)
SHIELD (Genesis 15:1)
SONG (Exodus 15:2, Isaiah 12:2)
SON OF GOD (Matthew 27:54)
SON OF MAN (Matthew 8:20)
SON OF THE MOST HIGH (Luke 1:32)
SOURCE (Hebrews 5:9)
SPIRIT (John 4:24)
SPIRIT OF ADOPTION (Romans 8:15)
SPIRIT OF GOD (Genesis 1:2)
SPIRIT OF TRUTH (John 14:17,15:26,16:13)
STRENGTH (Jeremiah 16:19)
STRONGHOLD (Nahum 1:7)
STRONG TOWER (Proverbs 18:10)
SUN OF RIGHTEOUSNESS (Malachi 4:2)

TEACHER (John 13:13)
TEMPLE (Revelation 21:22)

APPENDIX A

THE ONE (Psalm 144:2,10)
TRUE LIGHT (John 1:9)
TRUE WITNESS (Revelation 3:14)
TRUTH (John 14:6)

VINE (John 15:5)

WALL OF FIRE (Zechariah 2:5)
WAY (John 14:6)
WISDOM OF GOD (1 Cor. 1:24)
WITNESS (Isaiah 55:4)
WONDERFUL (Isaiah 9:6)
WORD (John 1:1)
WORD OF GOD (Revelation 19:13)

This partial list was adapted from http://www.godisreal.today/names-of-god/

WHAT IS NOW TRUE OF YOU

(Identity, Authority, Privilege)

-Adopted as God's child
-Justified
-Received & celebrated over by God
-Not condemned
-Filled in him
-A temple of the Holy Spirit
-Sealed & given the Spirit as a guarantee
-In God's kingdom now
-Redeemed
-Forgiven
-Reconciled to God
-A branch in the Vine

APPENDIX A

-No longer at enmity with God
-Dead to sin, but alive to God
-Called according to his purpose
-At peace with God
-Assured God is for me
-Chosen
-Sent by Jesus as the Father sent him
-A Spirit-empowered witness
-A member of Christ's body with purpose
-God's workmanship created in Christ Jesus
-Confident of sure hope of resurrection

I AM ACCEPTED

I am God's child. (John 1:12)

I am Christ's friend. (John 15:15)

I have been justified. (Romans 5:1)

I am united with the Lord, and I am one spirit with Him (1Cor. 6:17)

I have been bought with a price. I belong to God. (1Cor 6:19,20)

I am a member of Christ's body. (1 Cor. 12:27)

I am a saint. (Eph. 1:1)

I have been adopted as God's child. (Eph. 1:5)

I have direct access to God through the Holy Spirit. (Eph. 2:18)

I have been redeemed and forgiven of all my sins. (Col. 1:14)

I am complete in Christ. (Col. 2:10)

I AM SECURE

I am free forever from condemnation. (Rom. 8:1,2)

I am assured that all things work together for good. (Rom. 8:28)

I am free from any condemning charges against me. (Rom. 8:31f)

I cannot be separated from the love of God. (Rom. 8:35f)

APPENDIX A

I have been established, anointed, and sealed by God. (2 Cor. 1:21,22)

I am hidden with Christ in God. (Col. 3:3)

I am confident that the good work that God has begun in me will be perfected. (Phil. 1:6)

I am a citizen of heaven. (Phil. 3:20)

I have not been given a spirit of fear but of power and a sound mind. (2 Tim. 1:7)

I can find grace and mercy in time of need. (Heb. 4:16)

I am born of God, and the evil one cannot touch me. (1 John 5:18)

I AM SIGNIFICANT

I am the salt and light of the earth. (Matt. 5:13,14)

I am a branch of the true vine, a channel of His life. (John 15:1,5)

I have been chosen and appointed to bear fruit. (John 15:16)

I am a personal witness of Christ's. (Acts 1:8)

I am God's temple. (1 Cor. 3:16)

I am a minister of reconciliation for God. (2 Cor. 5:17f)

I am God's co-worker (2 Cor. 6:1; 1 Cor. 3:9)

I am seated with Christ in the heavenly realm. (Eph. 2:6)

This list was adapted from *Living Free in Christ, Neil Anderson*

APPENDIX B

Take a look at these four idols that many others emerge and grow from. Then notice which of the 4 Gs sets us free from this idol[10].

CONTROL
Desire: Self-discipline, certainty, standards
Price We Will Pay: Overworked, Loneliness
Greatest Nightmare: Uncertainty
Others Often Feel: Condemned, pushed
Problem Emotion: Worry, fear

*God is Great...*so I don't have to be in control (of people or situations). Jesus was raised from the dead when it seemed that all was lost.

APPROVAL
Desire: Affirmation, love, relationship
Price We Will Pay: Inauthenticity, codependency
Greatest Nightmare: Rejection
Others Often Feel: Smothered
Problem Emotion: Insecurity

*God is Glorious...*so I don't have to fear others. Jesus took our rejection and earned us full approval before the Father.

COMFORT
Desire: Privacy, lack of stress, freedom, easy life
Price We Will Pay: Ineffectiveness, selfishness
Greatest Nightmare: Stress, demands, pain or loss
Others Often Feel: Hurt
Problem Emotion: Boredom, discontentment

*God is Good...*So I don't have to look elsewhere for my satisfaction. Jesus is the Father's greatest gift to us and he is enough.

POWER
Desire: Success, influence
Price We Will Pay: Burdened, responsibility
Greatest Nightmare: Humiliation, lack of respect
Others Often Feel: Used
Problem Emotion: Anger

*God is Gracious...*so I don't have to prove myself (to my self... to others...to God). Jesus gave up his authority and power on the cross to secure our position in the Kingdom.

APPENDIX C

The Circle

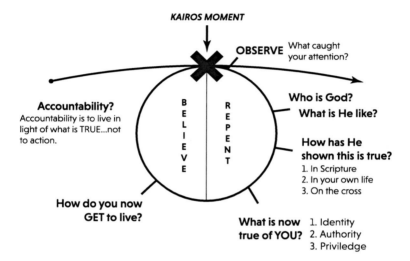

NOTE: *Kairos*: The word *kairos* is ised over 90 different times in the New Testament and having varying shades of meaning. The Greeks had two words for time. Chronos, where we get chronology from. This meant linear time–the days, weeks, months and years. And then there were *kairos* moments, divine moments. *Kairos* moments are those moments of epiphany, small or large that cause us to make decisions that shape our destiny. *Kairos* moments may be monumental, or they may be mundane, for God even speaks through a whisper. They may be moments of great joy, or they may be moments of great sorrow. Seeing your kairos moments is one thing, responding to them is yet another. We repsond to them by asking ourselves, what is God saying to me in the moment, and how does he want me to respond? The ability to see and respsond to our *kairos* moments in life is one of the paths to maturity. So what has been your *kairos* moment recently and how have you responded to it?

Repentence is not "feeling bad" about your choices or actions; it it turning from a pattern of unbelief and turning to belief in what is true of God and now true of you. Then we can act out of our new, restored beliefs!

ENDNOTES

1. I'm not sure who first coined this term, "gospel fluency", but I know that my friend and ministry partner for years, Jeff Vanderstelt, was one of the first people I heard use and give meaning to this phrase.

2. Caesar Kalinowski, *The Gospel Primer* (MissioPublishing.com) Week 1

3. Kenneth D. Boa and Robert M. Bowman, Jr., Faith Has It's Reasons, IVP Books   https://bible.org/seriespage/brief-history-apologetics p16

4. ibid

5. Tim Keller. *Doing Justice*. Resurgence Conference. Seattle. (2006). http://bit.ly/keller-dj

6. Caesar Kalinowski, The Gospel Primer (MissioPublishing.com) Week 1

7. Tim Chester, You Can Change: God's Transforming Power for Our Sinful Behavior and Negative Emotions, Crossway Books

    This powerful idea that all sin in our life comes from not believing one of these four eternal truths about God comes from Tim Chester and his book You Can Change. This has been a life-changing tool and way to speak the gospel into my life and the community I live in. Pretty much all of my thoughts on this you read here have come from Tim's teaching and conversations I've been blessed to have with him. I could not more highly recommend that you read his book and dig a whole lot deeper into this gospel truth. Thanks Tim!

8. Caesar Kalinowski, Small is Big, Slow is Fast (Grand Rapids, Zondervan, 2014) p65

9. Caesar Kalinowski, Small is Big, Slow is Fast (Grand Rapids, Zondervan, 2014) p77

10. Tim Keller, Preaching to the Heart. The Gospel Coalition National Conference, Orlando, Florida 2015

More From Caesar Kalinowski

TRANSFORMED
A New Way of Being Christian

Drawing on stories from Caesar's own journey and life in community, *Transformed* looks realistically at the identity you have been given in Christ and how it reshapes everything about you. Set free from performance-driven spirituality and guilt, you will draw closer to God, allowing him to radically change the well-worn rhythms and patterns of your every day life and transform your relationships from the inside out.

Easily available at: bit.do/transformed-book or on Amazon

SMALL IS BIG, SLOW IS FAST
Living And Leading Your Family And Community On God's Mission

Biblical and super practical, *Small Is Big, Slow Is Fast* by Caesar Kalinowski helps readers respond to Jesus' call to each of us to be a missionary right where we live—in our own families and neighborhoods. It shows you step-by-step the essential elements that create environments for organic kingdom growth and multiplication.

Easily available at: bit.do/small-is-big or on Amazon

Additional Resources For Your Journey

We also recommend these other books from Missio Publishing.

THE GOSPEL PRIMER

An 8-week Guide to Transformation in Community

by Caesar Kalinowski

Many in our churches have spent years listening to sermons, studying theology and reading the Word of God, yet still feel intimidated or unable to naturally express the good news of the Gospel into normal life, conversations, and circumstances.

In community, over 8 weeks, *The Gospel Primer* will help you creatively learn: What is the Gospel? We'll look at The Story of God that illustrates the gospel throughout all of scripture. You'll learn how to form and tell your personal 'My Gospel Story' in a natural, yet powerful way. We'll also look at how the Gospel has actually given us a new identity in Christ and how to live out the truth of this gospel identity in the normal rhythms of everyday life. We know of no other resource that can help you gain such a useable understanding and practice of the Gospel in such a short period of time.

THE TANGIBLE KINGDOM PRIMER
An 8-week Guide to Incarnational Community

by H. Halter and M. Smay

The Tangible Kingdom Primer is designed to help Christians, churches, and small groups get on the pathway of spiritual formation and missional engagement. This primer creates opportunities to experience authentic missional community step-by-step. It leads participants on a challenging 8-week journey toward an incarnational lifestyle and moves far beyond the typical small group experience. *The TK Primer* is a great starting point when trying to transition existing small groups toward more incarnational and missional rhythms.

THE JUSTICE PRIMER
An 8-week Guide to Serving through Community

by Brandon Hatmaker
Everyone's talking about social action and justice in the world. And for the first time in a long while, the Western church is looking for something designed to collectively point people outward and to give them a platform to do so together in community.

The Justice Primer is designed to be your guide on the journey of "learning to do right." It leads participants on a practical 8-week journey to put mission back into your small group or faith community. It's designed to help existing groups and churches begin or continue their journey toward being missional. If you desire to relearn the posture required to become missionaries in your context, and to equip others to engage culture through engaging the needs around them, *The Justice Primer* is your pilot.

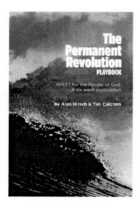

THE PERMANENT REVOLUTION PLAYBOOK

APEST for the People of God: A Six Week Exploration

by A. Hirsch and T. Catchim

There is clear guidance from Scripture itself as to how the church can be the fullness of Christ in the world. A vital part of the answer to a renewed ministry matching the challenges we face, is found in Eph.4:1-16. *The Permanent Revolution Playbook* by Alan Hirsch and Tim Catchim is designed to introduce individual disciples or teams to their own, Jesus-given, vocational profile.

BIVO

*A Modern Day Guide for
Bi-Vocational Saints*

by Hugh Halter

The Gospel came to us through fully paid, barely paid, and mostly non-paid saints. The future of Kingdom life and ministry depends on God's people to finding creative pathways for leveraging all of life into one calling. *BiVO* by Hugh Halter is a story and a framework to help you find this leverage point whether you are a marketplace leader or ministry leader.

These books are all available at: missiopublishing.com

Missio Publishing is committed to resourcing the church with practical tools to help it engage more effective;y in missional and incarnational ministry. To purchase the Primers and our other resources, along with bulk discounts, visit www.missiopublishing.com